Written by Clive Gifford.
Illustrations by Steve James.
Cover artwork based on designs by Thy Bui.

First published in Great Britain in 2022 by Red Shed, part of Farshore

An imprint of HarperCollins*Publishers*
1 London Bridge Street, London SE1 9GF
www.farshore.co.uk

HarperCollins*Publishers*
1st Floor, Watermarque Building, Ringsend Road
Dublin 4, Ireland

Copyright © HarperCollins*Publishers* Limited 2022

ISBN 978 0 00 856220 5

Printed and bound in the UK using 100% Renewable Electricity at CPI Group (UK) Ltd.

001

A CIP catalogue record for this title is available from the British Library.

MIX
Paper | Supporting
responsible forestry
FSC™ C007454

This book is produced from independently certified FSC™ paper
to ensure responsible forest management.

For more information visit: www.harpercollins.co.uk/green

AMAZING PUZZLES & QUIZZES

FOR EVERY 10 YEAR OLD

RED SHED

Have fun cracking clues and tackling quizzes with this puzzle book!

You'll find loads of fun questions and exciting brain teasers to challenge yourself with – or you can test your friends and family for hours of fun together!

Along the way, you'll find a mix of all sorts of puzzles – spot the difference, anagrams, quizzes, mazes and more. Each puzzle has instructions at the top of the page that tell you what you need to do. Once you've got your answer, or if you get stuck, head to the back of the book to check the solution.

Lets get started!

Mirror Match

Only one of the labelled images on this page is an exact mirror image of this shoe – all of the rest have small differences.

Can you work out which shoe is the mirror image?

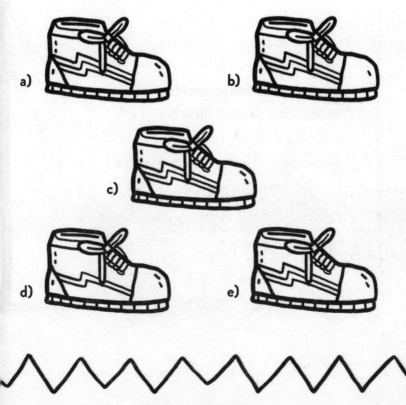

a)

b)

c)

d)

e)

Amazing Animals

1. **Which of these creatures has ears on its front legs, just below its knees?**

a) Chameleon   **b)** Cricket   **c)** Frog

2. **Which monkey, whose name is another word for 'nose', has a nose that can grow to around 17cm long?**

a) Proboscis
b) Howler
c) Marmoset

3. **Rats are ticklish and giggle when they're tickled. True or false?**

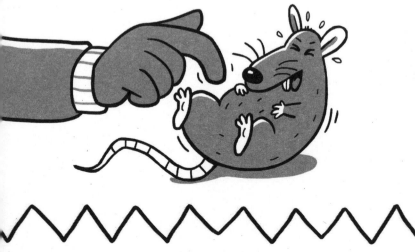

Answers on page 75

Make a Match: City Confusion

Eight cities, each made up of two words, have been jumbled up below. Can you match one word from the left-hand column with the correct word from the right-hand column to restore the city names?

Cape	York
Saint	Angeles
Buenos	Ababa
Santa	Town
Los	Aires
Mexico	Petersburg
New	Monica
Addis	City

Continental Challenges

I. **What is the biggest continent in the world?**

a) Asia
b) North America
c) Europe

2. **Which continent includes the capital cities of Santiago, Asunción and Lima?**

a) South America
b) Asia
c) Europe

3. **Which continent contains the largest number of countries?**

a) Asia
b) Africa
c) Europe

Answers on page 76

Follow the Line: Tech Tangle

These electronic devices have got their cables in a tangle!
Can you follow the lines to work out which plug
belongs with which device?

Large and Small

1. Around how long does it take to clean all
    the windows of the Burj Khalifa skyscraper
    in Dubai, the tallest building in the world?

    a) 12 hours   **b)** 4 days   **c)** 3 months

2. The world's smallest playable guitar is the size
    of an average adult man's little finger. True or false?

3. The world's smallest working prison, on the island
    of Sark off the coast of France, can hold only
    two prisoners. True or false?

4. The Tsar Bell, located in Moscow, Russia,
    is the largest bell in the world – but it has never
    been rung. True or false?

Answers on page 76

Make a Match: Collective Nouns

A collective noun is a naming word that describes a group of things, people or animals – such as 'a pride of lions'. **Eight collective nouns** have been mixed up below. Can you match the collective nouns in the left-hand column with the correct animal from the right-hand column?

A rhumba of . . .   monkeys

A sneak of . . .   apes

A gaggle of . . .   ravens

A barrel of . . .   tigers

A plague of . . .   weasels

A shrewdness of . . .   geese

An unkindness of . . .   locusts

An ambush of . . .   rattlesnakes

Answers on page 76

Eccentric Europe

1. In which country are 120 tonnes of tomatoes thrown in an hour-long enormous food fight called *La Tomatina*?

a) France
b) Spain
c) Finland

2. In which country can you find the cities of Stockholm and Gothenburg, as well as the *Nasoteket* (Nose Academy) – a museum dedicated to the noses of famous people?

a) Belgium   b) Slovenia   c) Sweden

3. Which tiny landlocked country, bordered by France and Spain, has a free postal system for letters sent within the country?

a) Lithuania
b) Andorra
c) Malta

Haunted Maze

Can you help the knight find a path through this maze from the start to the finish, and find the golden cup?

Tech Talk

1. The World Wide Web, created by Tim Berners-Lee in 1989, was nearly called 'The Information Mine'. True or false?

2. What is the name of the units that digital images are divided up into?

a) Pixels   **b)** Pieces   **c)** Icons

3. Over 180 million emails are sent every minute. True or false?

Cryptic Coding: Secretive Seas

An easy way to code messages is to swap letters for numbers. In one letter-number code, each letter in the alphabet is numbered in order, so A=1, B=2, C=3 etc, until you reach Z=26. Can you follow this code to decipher **five seas around the world** that are hidden below?

18 5 4

14 15 18 20 8

25 5 12 12 15 23

2 1 12 20 9 3

13 5 4 9 20 5 18 18 1 14 5 1 14

Try making up your own code messages using the same system and see if your friends and family can crack them!

Food for Thought

I. **Chorizo, kielbasa and Cumberland are all types of what sort of food?**

a) Pasta   **b)** Sausage   **c)** Bread roll

2. **What is shepherd's pie traditionally made from?**

a) Lamb mince topped with mashed potato
b) Roast chicken topped with potato slices
c) Fried leeks topped with breadcrumbs

3. **The biggest lasagne ever made weighed around one tonne, about the weight of one black rhinoceros. True or false?**

Answers on page 78

Blended Words: Sporty Pairs

Can you untangle the letters in each line below to reveal **eight sports**? On each line, two different sports with the same number of letters have been blended together, without changing the letter order in either sport. A clue is given below each pair to help you.

For example, JUDO and GOLF could be blended to create J**GO**U**L**DO**F**. It might help to jot down some notes on a piece of paper.

1. TBEONNXIINSG
One of these is played with a racquet, the other in a ring

2. SHKOICIKENGY
A winter sport and a sport that has 'ice' and 'field' versions

3. ACRRCIHCKEERTY
One of these needs a bow and arrow, the other needs a bat

4. BFAOOSTEBBAALLLL
Both of these are team sports – one involves a pitcher, the other a striker

Answers on page 78

The Human Body

1. **If an adult human's blood vessels were laid out in a long line from end to end, they would stretch exactly halfway around the world. True or false?**

2. **Which of these statements about height is true?**

a) You are taller in the morning than the evening
b) You are taller in the evening than the morning
c) You are the same height all the time

3. **What's the hardest substance in your body?**

a) Tooth enamel
b) Rib bones
c) Toenails

 Answers on page 79

Secret Scribbler: Brilliant Books

Someone has scribbled out some of the letters from these well-known books. Can you work out which letters are missing to reveal what they are? A clue is given below each entry. You might find it useful to jot them down on a piece of paper.

◆H◆ ◆O◆DE◆F◆L W◆Z◆◆D
◆F ◆Z

A girl from Kansas ends up following a yellow brick road

T◆E ◆U◆G◆E ◆O◆K

A story including the characters Mowgli, Baloo and Shere Khan

C◆A◆L◆T◆E'◆ ◆E◆

A story of a friendship between a spider and a pig called Wilbur

◆A◆E◆S◆I◆ D◆W◆

A story about Fiver, Hazel and other rabbits

◆H◆ S◆C◆E◆ ◆A◆DE◆

The story of a girl called Mary who grows to love nature

Talented Creatures

I. **Which of these creatures is the closest living relative to Tyrannosaurus?**

a) Crocodile   **b)** Bear   **c)** Chicken

2. **A koala bear can sleep for 18 hours a day. True or false?**

3. **The goliath frog weighs as much as an adult beagle dog. True or false?**

4. **Which African animal, found near rivers and lakes, makes its own sunscreen by secreting a red, oily substance over its body?**

a) Hippopotamus
b) Rhinoceros
c) Cape buffalo

Cryptic Coding: Terrific Trees

An easy way to code messages is to swap letters for numbers. In one letter-number code, each letter in the alphabet is numbered in order, so A=1, B=2, C=3 etc, until you reach Z=26. Can you follow this code to decipher the **five types of tree** below?

15 1 11

16 9 14 5

2 5 5 3 8

12 1 18 3 8

23 9 12 12 15 23

US States

1. Which of these is the largest state (by land area) in the United States of America?

a) Texas   **b)** California   **c)** Alaska

2. Which state became the 50th to join the United States of America in 1959?

a) Montana   **b)** Vermont   **c)** Hawaii

3. The US state of Minnesota's official state toy is silly putty . . .

True or False?

Riddle Time: Who Am I?

Can you find the answer to this riddle
using the clues on each line?

My first is in PEACHES but not in CHEAP,

My second is in PUSHES but never in SHEEP,

My third is in TRUMPET, MIGHT and WHIM,

My fourth is in TERM and also in SWIM,

My fifth is in EXCELLENT, three times in all,

My sixth is in CRICKET and also in BRAWL.

What am I?
Turn the book upside-down for a hint . . .

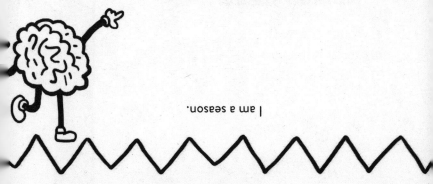

I am a season.

Desert Data

1. In 2011, Reza Pakravan crossed the whole Sahara desert on a bicycle in just 13 days, 6 hours. True or false?

2. How tall was the world's tallest homegrown cactus, at the point it was measured in 2015?

   a) 14.5m   **b)** 33.5m   **c)** 50.5m

3. On which continent can you find the Sahara, Kalahari and Namib deserts?

   a) Africa
   b) South America
   c) Oceania

4. How much of planet Earth's land surface is desert?

   a) About one-sixth
   b) About one-quarter
   c) About two-thirds

Secret Scribbler: Fabulous Food

Someone has come along and cheekily scribbled out alternate letters from these **five well-known foods and meals**. Can you work out what they are? A clue is given below each entry. You might find it useful to jot them down on a piece of paper.

F●S● A●D ●H●P●
You might have this wrapped in newspaper at the seaside

C●E●S● O● T●A●T
A popular snack made under the grill

A●P●E ●R●M●L●
A warm pudding, often served with custard

C●O● ●E●N
A Chinese noodle dish

●O●D ●N ●H● H●L●
A dish made with sausages and Yorkshire pudding

Spot the Difference: Fun at the Fair

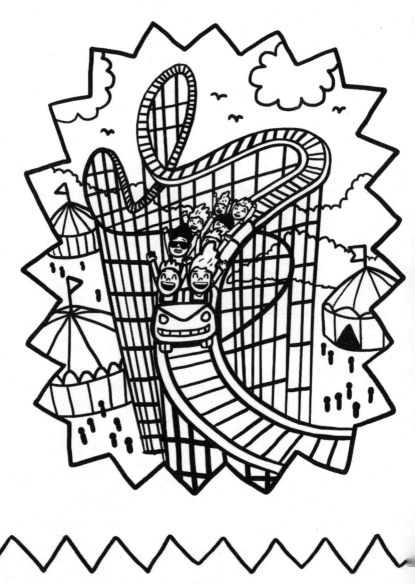

Answers on page 81

There are ten differences to spot between these two images. Can you find them all?

Working in Space

1. **Whilst performing a spacewalk, Heidemarie Stefanyshyn-Piper let go of a toolbag worth $100,000 that floated away and orbited Earth for several months all on its own. True or false?**

2. **On the International Space Station, wee is cleaned and recycled into drinking water. True or false?**

3. **What is a 'vomit comet'?**

a) An aircraft that flies up and down sharply to simulate weightlessness but makes some people feel sick.

b) A mysterious comet that made astronauts on the Moon sick when it flew past in 1969.

c) The nickname given to rocket launches, as they're so powerful they can make you feel ill.

Secret Scribbler: Global Landmarks

Someone has taken away some of the letters
from these **five well-known landmarks** from around the
world. Can you work out which letters are missing to
reveal what they are? A clue is given below each entry
to help you. You might find it useful to jot them
down on a piece of paper.

T✦E ✦I✦FE✦ ✦O✦E✦
A tall, steel structure in Paris

M✦C✦U ✦I✦C✦U
An Inca town built on a mountain peak in Peru

✦H✦ S✦A✦U✦ ✦F ✦I✦E✦TY
A copper goddess standing in New York harbour

✦Y✦N✦Y O✦E✦A ✦OUS✦
An Australian arts and music centre

M✦U✦T ✦U✦H✦O✦E
A mountain face carved with the heads
of four US presidents

All Action

I. **What country does the martial art, aikido, come from?**

a) Spain   **b)** India   **c)** Japan

2. **Slovenia's Davo Karnicar climbed Mount Everest then skied all the way down from the top. True or false?**

3. **What is the name of the person who performs fight scenes instead of a particular actor in a film?**

a) A stunt double
b) A danger devil
c) A doppelganger

Riddle Time: What Am I?

Can you find the answer to this riddle using the clues on each line?

My first is in CRAB but not in PRACTICE,

My second is in APPLE but not in PEOPLE,

My third is in the middle of MUSIC,

My fourth is in FIRE and also in LIGHT,

My fifth is in PLASMA but not in SPAMS.

What am I?
Turn the book upside-down for a hint...

I am a type of herb.

Miscellaneous Musings

1. Henri Matisse's painting, *Le Bateau* was hung upside-down by mistake in New York's Museum of Modern Art. How long do you think it took for anyone to notice?

    a) Three days **b)** Two weeks **c)** Six weeks

2. On a standard six-sided dice, what number do opposites sides always add up to?

    a) 4 **b)** 7 **c)** 9

3. Every human's tongue is different, like our fingerprints. True or false?

4. The world's most expensive coffee is made from coffee fruits that are eaten then pooed out by the Asian civet wild cat. True or false?

Answers on page 83

Bacteria

1. **How many different species of bacteria can be found in your mouth?**

   a) Around 25
   b) Around 700
   c) Around 5,000

2. **There are more bacteria cells in your body than human cells. True or false?**

3. **Bacteria have only been around since the dinosaurs died out. True or false?**

Jigsaw: Tropical Treetops

Two pieces are missing from this jigsaw! Can you work out which two of the puzzle pieces below fit exactly into the empty spaces opposite to complete the image? The correct pieces will need rotating.

a)

b)

c)

d)

e)

f)

g)

h)

Answers on page 83

Mammals

1. The American bison is North America's heaviest land animal. True or false?

2. Which of these creatures is a favourite food of polar bears? The bears can smell them from over 1,000m away – around ten football pitches!

a) Jellyfish   b) Fox   c) Seal

3. Polar and grizzly bears occasionally breed, producing a grolar bear. True or false?

4. A single blue whale weighs the same amount as about 500 people. True or false?

Secret Scribbler: Super Space

Someone has cheekily taken away alternate letters from these **five objects found in space**. Can you work out which letters are missing to reveal what they are? A clue is given below each entry to help you.

P ✦ A ✦ E ✦

For example, Mercury, Uranus or Earth

✦ S ✦ E ✦ O ✦ D

A large, rocky or metallic object in space

✦ P ✦ C ✦ S ✦ A ✦ I ✦ N

A place where astronauts live and work

✦ A ✦ E ✦ L ✦ T ✦

An object that orbits around a planet, such as Earth's Moon

✦ L ✦ C ✦ H ✦ L ✦

A mysterious, dark place in space

Shocking Animals

1. **Which creature, found in Africa, spins its tail like a fan whilst pooing to spray its poo long distances?**

a) Hippopotamus
b) Iguana
c) Wallaby

2. **A Siamese cat called Katy weighed 23kg – about the same as a 7 year old girl. True or false?**

3. **Which fierce hunter, the size of a medium dog and native to an island off the south coast of Australia, can eat 40% of its bodyweight in just half an hour?**

a) Wolverine
b) Tasmanian Devil
c) Coyote

Answers on page 84

What's the Job?

Can you answer these questions all about jobs? The number of letters in each solution is given in brackets.

Which 'C' is a person who makes delicious dishes in a restaurant? (4)

Which 'F' is a person who grows crops or tends livestock? (6)

Which 'D' is someone who looks after people's teeth and gums? (7)

Which 'S' is a person who performs operations in hospitals? (7)

Which 'A' is a person who designs buildings, bridges and other structures? (9)

Word Wonders

1. **Which one of the following words did William Shakespeare NOT invent?**

Downstairs   Eyeball   Fashionable
Gossip   Murder   Traditional

2. **There's no word in the dictionary that rhymes with orange. True or false?**

3. **Which of these do you think is the correct definition for the word 'qualtagh', a dialect word from the Isle of Man?**

a) The first person you see after you leave your home
b) The very last blob of toothpaste squeezed from a tube
c) The wig worn by a judge in court

Solar System

1. The Sun is so large that Earth could fit into it 1,300,000 times over. True or false?

2. Which of these is a dwarf planet named after the Greek god of the underworld, a name suggested by an 11-year-old schoolgirl from Oxford?

   a) Makemake   **b)** Pluto   **c)** Ceres

3. The planet Saturn has a moon that is larger than the planet Mercury. True or false?

4. Which is the hottest planet in our Solar System?

   a) Venus
   b) Mercury
   c) Mars

Riddle Time!

Can you work out the answers to these riddles?

1. What has no voice of its own, but will reply if spoken to?

2. A taxi driver was heading down a main road. She passed two red lights without stopping and watched a video on her phone, but didn't break any laws. Why?

3. I have thousands of words, but I cannot speak. What am I?

4. I can travel hundreds of kilometres around the world, without ever leaving my corner. What am I?

Answers on page 86

Big Business – True or False?

Can you work out which of these four statements about business are true or false?

1. The Google search engine was originally called 'AskAnyQuestion'. True or false?

2. The UK is home to more billionaires than any other country. True or false?

3. LEGO® makes more tyres than any other company in the world. True or false?

4. The largest collection of business cards in the world is owned by twin sisters in India, who have over 55,000 cards. True or false?

Exciting Elephants

1. **An elephant's trunk is powerful enough to lift around how many 40kg people?**

a) 2   b) 8   c) 20

2. **Elephants use their trunks as snorkels if they are in deep water. True or false?**

3. **There is only one species of African elephant. True or false?**

4. **Elephants can be left- or right-tusked, similarly to humans being left- and right-handed. True or false?**

Anagrams: Australian Animals

Can you unscramble the letters on each line to reveal **seven Australian animals**? The first letter of each word is in bold, to help you.

ORGANOA**K**

O**K**LAA

YL**P**AUTPS

DNOGI

OB**W**MTA

OS**P**SUM

ROOA**K**KURBA

World of Dinosaurs

1. **Which of these people was an expert fossil hunter, who lived from 1799–1847 and discovered skeletons of dinosaurs, including Plesiosaurus and Ichthyosaurus?**

a) Charles Darwin
b) Mary Anning
c) Rosalind Franklin

2. **Which dinosaur, named after the country in South America where its remains were found, grew up to 35m long and weighed around 10 times as much as a Tyrannosaurus?**

a) Argentinosaurus
b) Apatosaurus
c) Diplodocus

3. **Adult humans have around 32 teeth, but Edmontosaurus was a plant-eating dinosaur with around 1,000 teeth! True or false?**

Blended Words: Perfect Produce

Can you untangle the letters in each line below to reveal **four fruits and four vegetables**? On each line, a fruit and a vegetable with the same number of letters have been blended together, without changing the letter order in either word. A clue is given below each pair to help you.

For example, LIME and LEEK could be blended to create **LLIEMEEK**. It might help to jot down some notes on a piece of paper.

1. POENAIOCNH
One of these has a stone in its centre

2. OCRAARRNOGTE
These are both the same colour

3. ASPPIRINCACOHT
One of these is a dark green, leafy vegetable

4. CARSANPBAERARRGUSY
One of these is a bright red colour, and often used in juice

Money Matters

I. The island of Palau has produced a $5 coin that includes a scratch and sniff panel that smells of coconuts. True or false?

2. The first paper money was developed in the UK. True or false?

3. Which one of the following did the Aztecs NOT use as money?

a) Gold bars
b) Cocoa beans
c) Copper tools

4. Which of these famous figures has their face featured on a £50 UK bank note?

a) Jane Austen (novelist)
b) Horatio Nelson (navy commander)
c) Alan Turing (mathemetician)

Broken Pieces

Pickles the cat keeps pushing crockery off the shelf! Some of the vases have been broken beyond repair, but two of the pieces below fit together to make a complete vase matching the one on the shelf below. Can you find them?

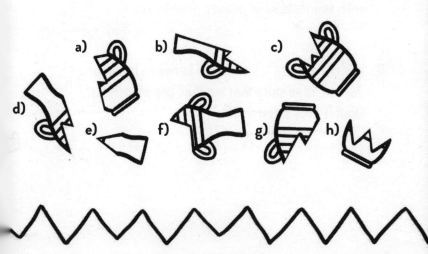

a)

b)

c)

d)

e)

f)

g)

h)

Salty Stuff

1. **Which country, bordering Peru, Chile and Brazil, is home to the world's biggest salt flats, that cover an area around the size of the island of Jamaica?**

a) Saudi Arabia   **b)** Mexico   **c)** Bolivia

2. **How much of a typical adult person's body is salt?**

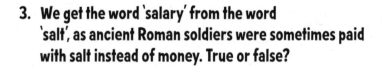

a) Less than 2 teaspoons
b) About 20 teaspoons
c) More than 40 teaspoons

3. **We get the word 'salary' from the word 'salt', as ancient Roman soldiers were sometimes paid with salt instead of money. True or false?**

4. **Which of these lakes, found between Israel and Jordan, is so salty that humans can effortlessly float if they swim in it?**

a) The Dead Sea   **b)** Lake Superior   **c)** Lake Como

Answers on page 88

Laboratory Maze

Can you find a path through this maze from the start to the finish, to help the scientist find their way back to their experiment?

Intriguing Inventions – True or False?

Can you work out which of these statements about amazing inventions are true or false?

1. The Viva Anywhere is a two-person road vehicle that can dive up to 10m underwater and fly short distances using rotor blades.

2. The first electric car was called the Maxim One, and had a range of just 500m – the length of its cord and plug.

3. In Japan, you can find a wearable robot called Tomatan that feeds you tomatoes.

4. A hat with an inbuilt radio was developed in the 1940s so that people could listen to the radio on the move.

Riddle Time: What Am I?

Can you find the answer to this riddle
using the clues on each line?

My first is in ASK but not in LACK,

My second is in PICK but not in PACK,

My third is in CLOSED and also in PLIGHT,

My fourth is in VOMIT, REVEAL and VASE,

My fifth is in MESS but not in CALMS,

My last is at the start of RETURN.

What am I?
Turn the book upside-down for a hint . . .

I am a type of metal.

Prehistoric Reptiles

1. **Which prehistoric flying reptile had a 2.5m-long head and 11m wingspan – the size of a fighter plane?** *Hint: it is also named after an Aztec feathered god.*

a) Pterodactylus
b) Quetzalcoatlus
c) Airlinersaurus

2. **Which sea-dwelling prehistoric reptile, whose name means 'eye lizard', had eyes the size of a netball?**

a) Ocularus
b) Imsurehesaurus
c) Ophthalmosaurus

3. **An Ichthyosaur prehistoric marine reptile was discovered in Canada that was about as long as a tennis court. True or false?**

Fears and Phobias

Can you match the name of each common phobia in the left-hand column to the fear in the right-hand column?

Arachnophobia	Fear of the number 8
Arithmophobia	Fear of small things
Octophobia	Fear of paper
Papyrophobia	Fear of spiders
Microphobia	Fear of animals
Zoophobia	Fear of numbers

Answers on page 90

Olympic Games

1. **What sport are athletes Michael Johnson, Allyson Felix, Shelley-Ann Fraser-Pryce and Usain Bolt all known for?**

a) Pole vault   b) Sprinting   c) Swimming

2. **Which country won their first and second ever Olympic gold medals in 2016 and 2021, both in Rugby Sevens?**

a) Japan   b) Canada   c) Fiji

3. **How old was Kokona Hiraki when she won a silver medal in women's park skateboarding at the Tokyo Olympics in 2021?**

a) 12
b) 16
c) 42

Answers on page 90

Odd One Out

All of the images on this page are identical to one another – apart from one. Can you work out which jar is different to the rest?

a)

b)

c)

d)

e)

Ancient Egypt

1. There were around the same number of symbols in the ancient Egyptian hieroglyphic alphabet as there are in the modern English alphabet. True or false?

2. The Great Pyramid of Giza was the world's tallest building for over 3,700 years. True or false?

3. When mummifying a dead body, which one of the following did the ancient Egyptians NOT do?

    a) Pull the brain out through the nostrils then throw it away
    b) Remove the eyes before wrapping the mummy
    c) Store the stomach and liver in ceremonial jars

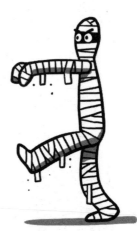

Answers on page 91

Cryptic Coding: Disguised Dogs

One easy way to code messages is to swap letters for numbers. In one letter-number code, each letter in the alphabet is numbered in order, so A=1, B=2, C=3 etc, until you reach Z=26. Can you follow this code to decipher the **five types of dog** that are hidden below?

16 21 7

2 15 24 5 18

8 21 19 11 25

19 16 1 14 9 5 12

3 15 12 12 9 5

Computing Questions

1. One early computer from the 1940s weighed around 30 tonnes. True or false?

2. Who is thought of as the world's first computer programmer?

a) Ada Lovelace, an English countess, mathematician and writer

b) Bill Gates, American businessman

c) Alan Turing, a mathematician and computer scientist

3. One Chinese supercomputer, *Tianhe-2*, uses around the same amount of electricity as 27,000 homes. True or false?

Follow the Line: Cool Cyclists

These cyclists have lost their bicycles! Can you follow the lines to work out which bicycle belongs with which cyclist?

Bird Bonanza

1. **Which bird can reach speeds of over 300km/h as it dives down to hunt?**

a) Heron
b) Turkey vulture
c) Peregrine falcon

2. **Which set of islands did Charles Darwin visit, finding several species of finch that helped him develop his theory of evolution?**

a) The Galapagos Islands
b) The Isles of Scilly
c) The Solomon Islands

3. **The vampire finch feeds by sucking blood from booby birds. True or false?**

Answers on page 92

Anagrams: Countries

Can you unscramble the letters on each line to spell out **five countries**? The capital city of each country is given beneath each anagram to help you.

CHAIN
Beijing

PAINS
Madrid

PLANE
Kathmandu

GRAYMEN
Berlin

RENTAGAIN
Buenos Aires

Terrific Trees

1. **In which country can you find Methuselah, a bristlecone pine tree believed to be over 4,800 years old?**

a) United States　　**b)** Scotland　　**c)** Croatia

2. **How many trees are there per person in Egypt?**

a) Around 70　　**b)** Around 10　　**c)** Around one

3. **There's an entire town of treehouses in Norway that are all 50m off the ground. True or false?**

4. **Trees share nutrients with each other using a special underground network made of fungi. True or false?**

Mirror Puzzle: Stripy Situation

Only one of the labelled images on this page is an exact mirror image of this zebra – all of the rest have small differences.

Can you work out which zebra is the mirror image?

a)

b)

c)

d)

e)

Gross Quiz

1. **How much mucus does the average person swallow every day?**

a) Around 0.5 litre
b) Around 1.5 litres
c) Around 3 litres

2. **Around how many times a day does the average person fart?**

a) 5   b) 15   c) 50

3. **The sweat and dirt from an ancient Greek athlete's bod was scraped off when they had finished exercising and sold as a pain-relief remedy. True or false?**

Blended Words: Confused Creatures

Can you untangle the letters in each line below to reveal **eight animals**? On each line, two animal names with the same number of letters have been blended together, without changing the letter order in either word. A clue is given below each pair to help you.

For example, LION and SEAL could be blended to create L S I E O A N L. It might help to jot down some notes on a piece of paper.

FBREAORG
One of these is an amphibian

SKNOAAKLAE
One of these is a marsupial

TSIHEGEERP
One of these has striped fur

BMAODNKGEERY
One of these is black and white

Smashing Sports

1. **What's the only Olympic sport where competitors compete while facing backwards?**

    a) Pentathlon   **b)** Bobsleigh   **c)** Rowing

2. **Ukrainian sportsman Sergey Bubka set 35 world records in just one event, which involves clearing a bar around 6m off the ground. What was it?**

    a) High jump
    b) 400m hurdles
    c) Pole vault

3. **Only one sport, so far, has been played on the Moon. What is it?**

    a) Golf   **b)** Long jump   **c)** Snooker

What's the Job?

Can you answer these five questions about jobs? The number of letters in each solution is given in brackets.

Which '**J**' is someone who sits in court and decides on cases? (5)

Which '**B**' is someone who cuts hair? (6)

Which '**P**' is a person who fixes water pipes and taps? (7)

Which '**M**' is someone who fixes cars and trucks? (8)

Which '**T**' is a person who converts words from one language to another? (10)

Answers on page 94

Curious Creatures

1. **Which of these animals does NOT shed its skin whole when it has outgrown it?**

   a) Grasshopper   **b)** Snake   **c)** Hedgehog

2. **Which of these creatures has its teeth in its stomach, its kidneys in its head and its brain in its throat?**

   a) Dust mite
   b) Lobster
   c) Tarantula spider

3. **One species of fairyfly only grows to 0.15mm long. True or false?**

4. **Duck-billed platypuses glow a blue-green colour when exposed to UV light. True or false?**

Answers on page 94

Secret Scribbler: Sailing Surprise

Someone has taken away some of the letters from these **six types of boat**. Can you work out which letters are missing to reveal what they are? A clue is given below each entry to help you. You might find it useful to jot them down on a piece of paper.

Y ❦ C ❦ T

A vessel with sails

❦ E ❦ R Y

A boat that carries passengers across a river, for example

D ❦ N ❦ H ❦

An inflatable boat

K ❦ Y ❦ K

A boat steered with a paddle with two blades

❦ O ❦ TA ❦ N ❦ R   ❦ H ❦ P

A boat that carries hundreds or thousands of standard-sized boxes

C ❦ U ❦ S ❦   L ❦ N ❦ R

A ship that carries lots of holidaymakers

Water, Water, Everywhere

1. **Which of these lakes can be found in the Great Lakes area of the USA?**

a) Windermere   **b)** Lake Superior   **c)** Loch Ness

2. **Italy, France, Greece and Tunisia all have coastlines on which one of these seas?**

a) Mediterranean
b) North
c) Yellow

3. **In Australia, you can find a lake called Lake Hillier, which has a bright pink colour. True or false?**

4. **Which of these lakes is the largest in Africa?**

a) Lake Malawi
b) Lake Victoria
c) Lake Titicaca

Intriguing Bakes and Bakers

1. *Jibachi senbei* is a type of cracker made in Japan containing which surprising ingredient?

a) A child's Wee
b) The bodies of wasps
c) Strips of cardboard

2. Joseph Pujol (1857–1945) was a French baker who opened a biscuit factory in later life. In between, he appeared on stage in front of kings and queens as what strange act?

a) A professional farter
b) A musician who burped tunes
c) A man who juggled working chainsaws

3. The longest cake ever made was exactly 1.6km long. True or false?

SOLUTIONS

Page 5: Mirror Match

The exact mirror image is **a**.

Page 6: Amazing Animals

1. b   **2.** a   **3.** True

Page 7: Make a Match: City Confusion

The eight cities are:
Cape Town
Saint Petersburg
Buenos Aires
Santa Monica
Los Angeles
Mexico City
New York
Addis Ababa

Page 8: Continental Challenges

1. a   **2.** a   **3.** b

Page 9: Follow the Line: Tech Tangle

1 with **b**, **2** with **d**, **3** with **a**, **4** with **c**

Page 10: Large and Small

1. c. There are over 24,000 windows!
2. False. It is actually much smaller, only about the size of a single red blood cell.
3. True
4. True

Page 11: Make a Match: Collective Nouns

The completed collective noun sentences are as follows:
A rhumba of rattlesnakes
A sneak of weasels
A gaggle of geese
A barrel of monkeys
A plague of locusts
A shrewdness of apes
An unkindness of ravens
An ambush of tigers

Page 12: Eccentric Europe

1. b   **2.** c   **3.** b

Page 13: Haunted Maze

Page 14: Tech Talk

1. True   **2.** a   **3.** True

Page 15: Cryptic Coding: Secretive Seas

In order, the seas are:
RED
NORTH
YELLOW
BALTIC
MEDITERRANEAN

Page 16: Food for Thought

1. b

2. a

3. False. It actually weighed around 4.8 tonnes and included 400kg of mozzarella and 500 litres of tomato sauce!

Page 17: Blended Words: Sporty Pairs

In the order they appear, the blended sports are:

1. TENNIS and BOXING
2. SKIING and HOCKEY
3. ARCHERY and CRICKET
4. BASEBALL and FOOTBALL

Page 18: The Human Body

1. False. They would actually stretch much further, about twice around the world.

2. a. You are taller in the morning because the cartilage in your body compresses over the day, making you slightly shorter by the time you go to bed.

3. a

Page 19: Secret Scribbler: Brilliant Books

In the order they appear, the books are:
THE WONDERFUL WIZARD OF OZ
THE JUNGLE BOOK
CHARLOTTE'S WEB
WATERSHIP DOWN
THE SECRET GARDEN

Page 20: Talented Creatures

1. c
2. True
3. False
4. a

Page 21: Cryptic Coding: Terrific Trees

In the order they appear, the trees are:
OAK
PINE
BEECH
LARCH
WILLOW

Page 22: US States

1. c **2.** c **3.** False

Page 23: Riddle Time: Who Am I?

Summer. The clues refer to the letters within the words on each line. For example, 'my first' refers to the first letter of the solution, 'S', which can be found in the word 'peaches' but not in 'cheap'. If you follow the clues down the list in the same way, you can spell out 'summer', a season.

Page 24: Desert Data

1. True **3.** a
2. b **4.** b

Page 25: Secret Scribbler: Fabulous Food

In the order they appear, the foods and meals are:

FISH AND CHIPS
CHEESE ON TOAST
APPLE CRUMBLE
CHOW MEIN
TOAD IN THE HOLE

Page 26: Spot the Difference: Fun at the Fair

Page 28: Working in Space

1. True   **2.** True   **3.** a

Page 29: Secret Scribbler: Global Landmarks

In the order they appear, the landmarks are:

THE EIFFEL TOWER
MACHU PICCHU
THE STATUE OF LIBERTY
SYDNEY OPERA HOUSE
MOUNT RUSHMORE

Page 30: All Action

1. c   **2.** True   **3.** a

Page 31: Riddle Time: Who Am I?

Basil. The clues refer to the letters within the words on each line. For example, 'my first' refers to the first letter of the solution, 'B', which can be found in the word 'cra<u>b</u>' but not in 'practice'. If you follow the clues down the list in the same way, you can spell out 'basil', a type of herb.

Page 32: Miscellaneous Musings

1. c   **3.** True
2. b   **4.** True

Page 33: Bacteria

1. b
2. True
3. False. They were among the first living things on Earth.

Page 34: Jigsaw: Tropical Treetops

The missing pieces are **g** and **c**.

Page 36: Mammals

1. True
2. c
3. True
4. False. They actually weigh as much as around 1,500 people!

Page 37: Secret Scribbler: Super Space

In the order they appear, the space words are:

PLANET
ASTEROID
SPACE STATION
SATELLITE
BLACK HOLE

Page 38: Shocking Animals

1. a   **2.** True   **3.** b

Page 39: What's the Job?

In the order they appear, the jobs are:
Chef
Farmer
Dentist
Surgeon
Architect

Page 40: Word Wonders

1. Murder
2. False. 'Sporange' is a real word, meaning a sac where spores are made in fungi and algae.
3. a

Page 41: Solar System

1. True
2. b
3. True. The moon is called Titan.
4. a

Page 42: Riddle Time!

1. An echo
2. She was walking down the road, not driving
3. A book
4. A stamp

Page 43: Big Business – True or False?

1. False. It was called BackRub.
2. False. Most billionaires can be found in the USA and China.
3. True
4. True

Page 44: Exciting Elephants

1. b
2. True
3. False. There are two species, savanna elephants and forest elephants.
4. True

Page 45: Anagrams: Australian Animals

In the order they appear, the animals are:
KANGAROO
KOALA
PLATYPUS
DINGO
WOMBAT
POSSUM
KOOKABURRA

Page 46: World of Dinosaurs

1. b   **2.** a   **3.** True

Page 47: Blended Words: Perfect Produce

In the order they appear, the word pairs are:
PEACH and ONION
ORANGE and CARROT
APRICOT and SPINACH
CRANBERRY and ASPARAGUS

Page 48: Money Matters

1. True
2. False. It was developed in China, during the Song dynasty.
3. a
4. c

Page 49: Broken Pieces

The two pieces that fit together are **d** and **g**.

Page 50: Salty Stuff

1. c   **3.** True
2. c   **4.** a

Page 51: Laboratory Maze

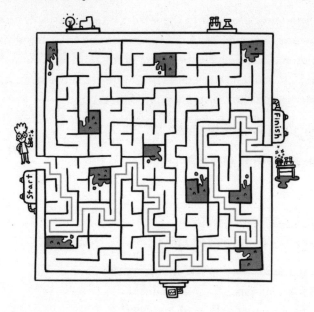

Page 52: Intriguing Inventions – True or False?

1. False
2. False
3. True
4. True

Page 53: Riddle Time: What Am I?

Silver. The clues refer to the letters within the words on each line. For example, 'my first' refers to the first letter of the solution, 'S', which can be found in the word 'ask' but not in 'lack'. If you follow the clues down the list in the same way, you can spell out 'silver', a type of metal.

Page 54: Prehistoric Reptiles

1. b.   **2.** c.   **3.** True

Page 55: Fears and Phobias

In the order they appear, the fears and phobias are:
Arachnophobia – Fear of spiders
Arithmophobia – Fear of numbers
Octophobia – Fear of the number 8
Papyrophobia – Fear of paper
Microphobia – Fear of small things
Zoophobia – Fear of animals

Page 56: Olympic Games

1. b   **2.** c   **3.** a

Page 57: Odd One Out

The odd one out is **a.**

Page 58: Ancient Egypt

1. False. There were more than 700!
2. True
3. b

Page 59: Cryptic Coding: Disguised Dogs

In the order they appear, the types of dog are:
PUG
BOXER
HUSKY
SPANIEL
COLLIE

Page 60: Computing Questions

1. True   **2.** a   **3.** True

Page 61: Follow the Line: Cool Cyclists

1 with **b**, **2** with **c**, **3** with **d**, **4** with **a**

Page 62: Bird Bonanza

1. c   **2.** a   **3.** True

Page 63: Anagrams: Countries

In the order they appear, the countries are:
CHINA
SPAIN
NEPAL
GERMANY
ARGENTINA

Page 64: Terrific Trees

1. a   **3.** False

2. c   **4.** True

Page 65: Mirror Puzzle: Stripy Situation

The exact mirror image is **d**.

a)

b)

c)

e)

Page 66: Gross Quiz

1. b

2. b

3. True

Page 67: Blended Words: Confused Creatures

In the order they appear, the animal pairs are:
FROG and BEAR
SNAKE and KOALA
TIGER and SHEEP
BADGER and MONKEY

Page 68: Smashing Sports

1. c **2.** c **3.** a

Page 69: What's the Job?

In the order they appear, the jobs are:
Judge
Barber
Plumber
Mechanic
Translator

Page 70: Curious Creatures

1. c **3.** True
2. b **4.** True

Page 71: Secret Scribbler: Sailing Surprise

In the order they appear, the boats are:
YACHT
FERRY
DINGHY
KAYAK
CONTAINER SHIP
CRUISE LINER

Page 72: Water, Water, Everywhere

1. b   **3.** True
2. a   **4.** b

Page 73: Intriguing Bakes and Bakers

1. b
2. a
3. False. It was actually 5.3km long!

Try the rest of the series to carry on the fun!